Paradigm

Sessions 1–120

KEYBOARDING

With

snap

User Guide

D1443974

EMCParadigm
PUBLISHING

www.keyboarding.emcp.com

PARADIGM KEYBOARDING WITH SNAP END USER LICENSE AGREEMENT

Paradigm Publishing, Inc. ("Paradigm") grants the "End User" (herein defined as any person who downloads the files associated with the Paradigm Keyboarding with Snap product, hereafter referred to as the "Program") permission to use both the files and content of the Program. By doing so the End User acknowledges that Paradigm holds all benefits of copyright in the aforementioned Product. The End User further agrees that the Product will not be copied, sold for profit, or redistributed in any manner to any third party for any reason whatsoever without the express written consent of Paradigm. The End User agrees that Paradigm, at its sole discretion, with, or without cause, may revoke this permission at any time. By using the enclosed password to enter Paradigm Keyboarding with Snap, the End User acknowledges having read and understood the terms of the User License and hereby agrees that they will comply with the terms of The End User License.

ISBN 0-7638-2309-0
C/N 02671

Published by EMC Corporation
875 Montreal Way
St. Paul, MN 55102
(800) 535-6865
E-mail: educate@emcp.com
Website: www.emcp.com

Printed in the United States of America
10 9 8 7 6 5 4 3 2

Contents

Welcome to Paradigm Keyboarding with Snap (PKB)

Welcome to Paradigm Keyboarding with Snap! With Paradigm Keyboarding with Snap (PKB) you can both enhance and demonstrate the keyboarding skills you are learning in your course. You will use PKB to take training sessions assigned by your instructor as part of your coursework. You can also use PKB to see the results of the work you do, to get course information, and to communicate with your instructor.

This User Guide serves as an introduction to the PKB interface and features. It also describes the functions of the Paradigm Word Processor (PWP) that comes with PKB.

Preparing Your Computer for PKB

PKB is a Web-based program available to you over the Internet at any time. The following are the minimum system requirements for using PKB on your computer:

- **Processor:** Intel Celeron 600Mhz or higher
- **Memory:** 128 MB minimum (256 MB highly recommended for Windows XP)
- **Operating System:** Windows XP Home/Professional (with SP1 or higher), Windows 2000 (with SP4)
- **Web Browser:** Internet Explorer 6.0
- **Web Browser Settings:**
  - Scripting and cookies enabled within Internet Explorer
  - Any pop-up blocking software disabled for keyboarding.emcp.com.
  - Browser configured to download and run signed ActiveX controls and plug-ins
- **Firewall Settings:** Firewall on your computer set to allow data transfer to and from keyboarding.emcp.com.
- **Screen Resolution:** 800 x 600 in 16 bit color
- **User Privileges for Installing ActiveX Control (first time only):**
  - Windows XP – Administrative privileges are required to install the ActiveX control for the first time.

○ Windows 2000 – Power user (or higher) privileges are required to install the ActiveX control for the first time.

To enable scripts and cookies in Internet Explorer, take the following steps:

1. Click Tools and then click Internet Options.

2. Click Privacy.

3. Select Medium on the Privacy slider.

4. Click OK.

To ensure that Active X controls and plug-ins are enabled in Internet Explorer, take the following steps:

1. Click Tools and then click Internet Options.

2. Click the Security Tab.

3. Select Internet from the list of zones displayed. The security level for this zone should be set at "Medium." If not, follow any of the methods mentioned below.

Method 1 - Utilizing the default Zone Security Settings (Recommended)

1. Click the Default Level button.

2. Click OK.

Method 2 - Customizing the Internet Zone Security Settings

1. Click the Custom Level button.

2. Navigate to the section entitled ActiveX controls and plug-ins.

3. Locate the heading entitled Download signed ActiveX controls and click Prompt.

> ☑ Download signed ActiveX controls
> ○ Disable
> ○ Enable
> ◉ Prompt

4. Locate the heading entitled Script ActiveX controls marked safe for scripting and click Enable.

> ☑ Script ActiveX controls marked safe for scripting
> ○ Disable
> ⊙ Enable
> ○ Prompt

5. Navigate to the section entitled Downloads.

6. Locate the heading entitled File download and click Enable.

> 🔄 File download
> ○ Disable
> ⊙ Enable

7. Navigate to the section entitled Scripting.

8. Locate the heading Active scripting and click Enable.

> 📝 Active scripting
> ○ Disable
> ⊙ Enable
> ○ Prompt

9. Click OK to save your changes.

10. Click OK again to shut the window.

Accessing PKB

Once you have prepared your computer, access PKB by taking the following steps:

1. Log on to the Internet if your computer is not already connected to it.

2. At the Windows desktop of your computer, double-click the *Internet Explorer* 🟦 icon.

3. At the Internet Explorer screen, click on the entry in the Address text box.

4. Key **www.keyboarding.emcp.com** in the Address text box and click *GO*. The Paradigm Keyboarding with Snap home page appears.

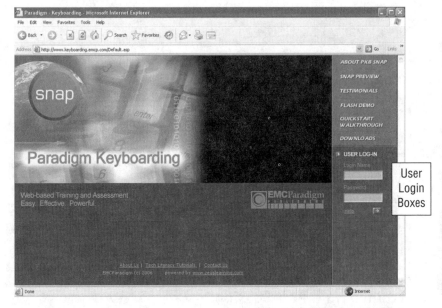

5. Your instructor has given you the login name that has been assigned for your class. On the inside front cover of the *User Guide* is your unique PKB password that you will use with the login name from your instructor to access PKB. Enter your login name in the Login Name text box (lower right corner of the screen). Enter your password in the Password text box.

6. Click the red arrow button.

Note: If you enter either your login name or password incorrectly, you will receive an error message, stating that you need to try again. You must re-type your login details exactly; login names and passwords are case sensitive. If you have forgotten your login name or password, please contact your instructor.

7. When you log into Paradigm Keyboarding for the first time, you will be asked to read and agree to the Paradigm Keyboarding with Snap End User License Agreement, and to verify certain details about your course. You will need to do this only once.

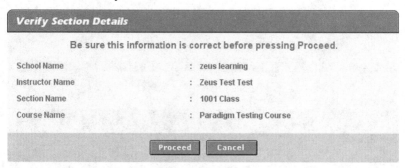

If the information displayed at this point is correct, click the Proceed button to continue.

Note: If the information displayed does not match your course details, click Cancel and contact your instructor to get the correct login name for your section. If you discover you are in the wrong section after you have already enrolled, ask your instructor to have you moved to the correct section.

Launching a PKB Session

Once you have logged in, your Paradigm Keyboarding with Snap Welcome page appears.

This page (also called the Home page) lists all exercises within the training sessions for your course, and also states which exercises you have taken. It also has the PKB menu bar with which you can navigate from page to page in PKB.

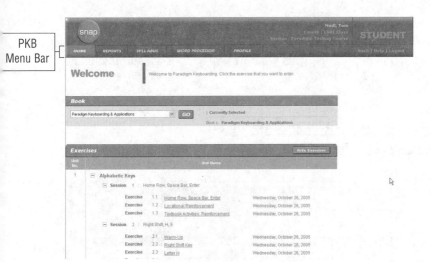

PKB
Menu Bar

Click an exercise title hyperlink to launch it. The Launch
Keyboarding dialog box is displayed. Click the Launch button to
launch Paradigm Keyboarding.

When you click the Launch button, a progress window is displayed
while the necessary resource files are downloaded. Once Paradigm
Keyboarding is launched, the following window is displayed.

This window remains open in the background while Paradigm Keyboarding is running. Do not close this window while the PKB session is in progress.This window will shut down automatically when you exit the PKB session.

Doing PKB Session Exercises

When the Launch process is complete, the PKB Exercise screen appears.

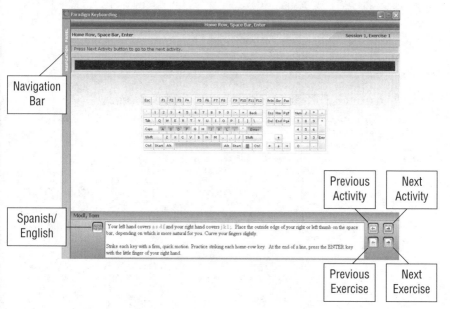

The PKB Sessions Screen

The PKB Sessions screen features the following buttons and functions:

Next Activity/Previous Activity 🔲 🔲 These buttons take you to the next or previous activity within an exercise.

Next Exercise/Previous Exercise 🔲 🔲 These buttons take you to the next or previous exercise of the program. These will provide the most common way of moving through the program.

Navigation Bar This feature allows you to move to any session and exercise within the program. Click on the orange panel with your mouse and a tree menu showing all of PKB's sessions and exercises appears.

Spanish/English This toggle button allows you to view most software instructions in Spanish. Click the button to see instructions in Spanish. Click it again to see them in English.

Close ☒ This button closes the Sessions screen and returns you to the Welcome page.

PKB provides hands-on experience in learning keyboarding and document formatting skills. Keyboarding instruction, practice, Timed Short Drills, and Thinking Drills are presented on the screen. Paragraph timings and word processing instruction are presented in the textbook. Production documents and timings are checked for accuracy and speed by PKB.

Error Checking and Marking in PKB

Many of the exercises in the software use a special text checker that gives feedback regarding how many errors you have made and also displays the location of each error. PKB compares your keyed work with a master document stored in the program. The program checks for the following kinds of errors:

- Misspelled words
- Missing words
- Spacing errors, including missing tabs and extra or missing spaces between words and between sentences
- Punctuation errors
- Capitalization errors

There may be rare instances, such as in a timing when a common word that should be capitalized isn't and then is repeated later on lowercase, when the checker will misread or skip text and thus give a high error count. This should not happen often.

Missing words are indicated with a caret (^) symbol. Joined-together words are followed by a caret (^). Misspelled or wrong words are highlighted or marked with a strikethrough line. For errors in punctuation or spacing (for example, sentences that end with two spaces instead of one space after a period), the checker flags the word preceding the error.

For all exercises with a time limit or for which the speed is displayed on the screen or on a printout, the clock will start only when the first key is struck.

Files Created by PKB

The text for all of the exercises, except Production and Timings, is automatically saved by PKB in a session file that may be printed out at a later time. This session transcript is called *xxx*ses.rtf, where *xxx* is the session number. For example, the practice and drills completed in the first session would be saved in a file called 001ses.rtf. Paragraph timings are saved by PKB in a timings file, called *xxx*tim.rtf, where *xxx* is the session number. Production documents are each named and saved as files as described in the textbook.

See the section on the View Submissions Report (p. 19) to learn how to access these files.

Exercise Types in PKB

Instructions will appear on screen for all exercise types. In those cases in which you need to follow instructions given in the textbook, you will be directed to do so by PKB. Not all exercise types appear in each session. What follows is a listing and description of the most common exercise types.

Warm-Up

This short exercise appears at the beginning of many sessions. Key each line as it appears, then press *Enter*.

Key Introduction

This exercise introduces a new key. It illustrates the proper fingering to use in striking the key and gives you an opportunity to practice the reach.

Drill Lines/ Sentences

This exercise usually occurs immediately after a key introduction. The program displays words or lines of text that incorporate the target key. You key the line, press *Enter*, then PKB displays a new line.

Locational Reinforcement

You are asked to key a short line of text. The software times you. You then key longer and longer lines of text, with a time limit of twice your original time, three times your original time, and so on.

Timings (Lines)

You key the line as shown on the screen. You are timed for the number of seconds displayed at the bottom of the screen. When you have keyed the line and pressed *Enter*, or when the time has expired, the attained speed is displayed.

Timings (Paragraph)

You will need to refer to the textbook to complete this type of exercise. The textbook page and exercise number are displayed at the top of the screen, along with the time allowed to complete the exercise. Key the material as it appears in the textbook. If you complete the material, start over (but do not key it more than twice during a single exercise). When time is up, your attained speed and errors will be displayed, as well as the location of each error. Note that if you make a spacing error, the word before the error is highlighted.

Speed Push/Accuracy Push

You are given the chance to practice a number of lines. You key each line as it appears, then press *Enter* at the end of each line. All of the lines keyed are displayed, and you are asked to choose which line you think you can key within the indicated time or can key without error within the indicated time. If you key the line within the time limit, you are given a chance to key the next longer line. If you don't finish, you get a chance to try the previous shorter line.

Timed Short Drills

In this exercise, a dialog box appears on screen. You choose to concentrate on either speed or accuracy. Then you choose the length of the Timed Short Drill you want (15, 30, or 60 seconds) and the speed level for which you wish to aim. You then key the drill displayed on screen. If you finish before time is up, you can start over, but don't do a drill more than twice. Your attained speed will be displayed, along with any errors.

If you have chosen the Speed setting, you must complete the drill at least once, at which time you are given a longer drill to key. If you don't complete the drill, PKB will have you repeat it. If you choose the Accuracy setting, you must complete the drill at least once with no more than one error, or else PKB will have you do it again. You can always change the settings and speed rates at the end of a drill by clicking the Start Over button. To leave Timed Short Drills, click the Next Exercise button.

Thinking Drills

These drills give you the opportunity to think about what should be keyed before keying it. You will need to key the correct word, phrase, or sentence based on the instructions provided. The software will show you any errors you may have made.

Numeric Timings

Numeric timings in Sessions 14-17 are done the same way as regular paragraph timings. Numeric timings in Sessions 24-27 are entered using the numeric keypad. In these sessions, the form looks like a grid or spreadsheet. When you have entered the numbers and time is up, PKB will list your WAM and number of errors, and display errors.

Textbook Activities: Reinforcement

Reinforcement exercises help you review the key reaches learned in a session using the textbook. You will be directed to the textbook for instructions. When you are finished, you can print your work from the screen using the Print 🖫 button, although you will have to add student information manually. Or, you can click Next Exercise, at which time PKB saves your work along with your student information as part of your session file (xxxses.rtf), which can be printed out in the Paradigm Word Processor (PWP).

Timing Feature

When you click the Timing 🔘 button at the bottom of the Word Processor screen, you will be asked to indicate the length of the timing you want to perform. Enter the length and whether it should be measured in seconds or minutes. Then click OK. The timing will begin when you start keying. You will be stopped when time is up. Your "words-a-minute" (WAM) score will then be indicated.

WAM Only Feature

Click the WAM 🔘 button to have the computer check your speed without imposing any time limit. Click the Stop WAM 🔘 button when you are finished, and your score will be displayed.

Production Documents

Production exercises feature those Production documents in the text that can be checked for accuracy by PKB (such as Document B in Session 45), and those that will be created in PWP but not checked (such as Document C in Session 45). When you begin the Production exercises, the session number and document letter are displayed on your screen. The textbook provides instructions for working with these exercises and for naming and saving them.

Keying Checked Production Documents

1. Key the document from the text, following the steps exactly.

2. When you are ready to have the document checked, click the Check 🔘 button near the bottom of your screen. This command automatically names and saves the document, checks it for errors, and calculates the WAM rate. In addition, the score is automatically recorded in your Production Performance Report. (See page 18.) Then the program displays the checked document on the screen. (Important: If you need a copy of the checked document with the errors highlighted, you must print the document while the checked version is shown on screen. If you print the production document at a different time, the errors will not be highlighted on the printout.)

3. After you have finished viewing the checked document, you may go back to the original document by clicking on the View Original 🔘 button near the bottom of the screen. If you correct the original document, you can recheck it (by clicking the Check button again), and your new WAM rate

will reflect the time you took to edit the document. The timer begins when you strike the first key of the change. You may bring your errors down to zero by editing your document, but your WAM rate also will be lower because more time will have been spent. **Note that the only WAM and error readings saved in the Production Performance Report are those from the initial keying of the document.**

You also have the ability to switch back and forth between the checked version and actual document by clicking View Original or View Checked. This allows you to compare your text with the version in which errors are marked.

You can print either the checked-text version or the regular version of a Production Document using File→Print. If you print the checked-text version, your name, ID number, and the date will automatically appear on the printout. You have to add this information manually, however, when printing the actual document.

6. **Do NOT close the file.** Exit the exercise by clicking on the Next Exercise button. The program will save the exercise appropriately for you, and go on to the next exercise.

Keying Production Documents That Are Not Checked

Documents created in PWP that are not checked are like regular word processing documents. You name and save the file manually, add any student information manually, and can close the file before clicking the Next Exercise button. PKB does not check these documents for errors, but does offer the Timing and WAM Only features for monitoring your speed. See the section on the Paradigm Word Processor (PWP) (p. 20) for more information.

Viewing Your PKB Reports and Files

PKB provides you with a variety of reports that show your performance and progress. You can view these reports from your PKB Welcome page by pointing to Reports on your PKB menu bar.

Progress Report

The Progress Report helps you keep track of your progress for all sessions within your course. To view the report, take the following steps:

1. At your PKB Welcome page, point to Reports and click Progress Report.

2. At the Student Progress Report Wizard, select the sessions for which you want to view the completion status. You can view the progress of up to ten sessions at a time.

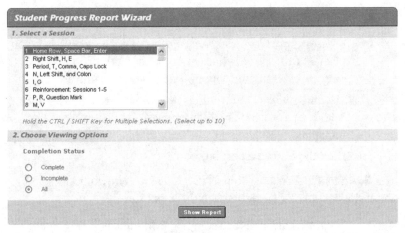

3. Select from the following viewing options:

   ☐ *Complete:* Selecting this option displays a list of completed sessions only.

   ☐ *Incomplete:* Selecting this option displays a list of incomplete sessions only.

   ☐ *All:* Selecting this option displays the completion status for all selected sessions.

4. Click the Show Report button. The Progress Report shows which exercises you have completed within the selected sessions.

   ☐ *Session Name:* Completed exercises within a session appear checked, and incomplete exercises appear crossed.

   ☐ *Status:* A check indicates that all exercises within a

session are complete. A cross indicates that at least one exercise within the session is incomplete or not attempted.

Timings Performance Report

In this report, you can view your best performances, based on highest WAM scores for the different types of timings exercises, namely, 1-Minute, 3-Minute, and 5-Minute. You can view this report by taking the following steps:

1. Point to Reports and click Timings Performance Report.

2. Select from the following viewing options:

   ☐ *Show report for 20 recent timings of each type.* When you select this option, your performance in the 20 most recently attempted timings exercises is displayed.

   ☐ *Show report for all timings.* When you select this option, your performance in all attempted timings exercises is displayed.

3. Click the Show Report button.

The Timings Performance Report displays the following information about the best performance in each timings exercise:

   ☐ *WAM:* Displays the typing speed in terms of words a minute. The Timings Performance Report always displays information about the attempt with the highest WAM score.

   ☐ *Errors:* Displays the number of errors in that attempt.

   ☐ *Document:* Click the <u>View Document</u> hyperlink to open your Timings file (*xxxtif*.rtf) for that session.

   ☐ *Show Graph:* Click the Show Graph button to view a graph of your performance across 20 recent timings exercises attempted.

Production Performance Report

The Production Performance Report helps you judge your ability to prepare lengthy documents like letters, memorandums, reports, or manuscripts. You can follow these steps to generate a report that summarizes your performance in the document preparation exercises. To view the Production Performance Report, take the following steps:

1. Point to Reports and click Production Performance Report.

2. Select from one of the following options:

   ☐ *Show report for 20 most recent documents.* When you select this option, details of your performance in the 20 most recent document preparation exercises attempted is displayed.

   ☐ *Show report for all documents.* When you select this option, details of your performance in all document preparation exercises attempted is displayed.

3. Click the Show Report button.

The Production Performance Report displays the following information about the document preparation exercises you have attempted:

   ☐ *WAM:* Displays your typing speed for the session in terms of words a minute.

   ☐ *Errors:* Displays the number of errors in the document.

   ☐ *Show Graph:* Click the "Show Graph" button to view a graph of your performance across 20 recent document preparation exercises.

   ☐ *Document:* You can view the document you have prepared in an exercise by clicking the document hyperlink.

Note: The Production Performance Report always displays details of your first attempt of the exercise only. If you reattempt a document preparation exercise, your performance will not be reflected in the report.

View Submissions Report

The View Submissions Report page allows you to view all session, timings, and/or production files you have submitted to your instructor on completion of various session exercises. The report will list the 20 most recently modified files for the selected option. To see the View Submissions Report, take the following steps:

1. Point to Reports and click Submissions Report.

2. At the Student View Submissions Report Wizard, select one of the following viewing options.

   ☐ *Show production files* or *Show unchecked production files.* Selecting this option displays documents submitted in the document preparation exercises.

   ☐ *Show timing files.* Selecting this option displays documents submitted in the timings exercises.

   ☐ *Show session files.* Selecting this option displays documents submitted in the session exercises.

   ☐ *Show all files.* Selecting this option displays documents submitted in all exercises.

3. Click the Show Report button.

The View Submissions Report lists the documents that have been submitted in various sessions.

   ☐ *File Type:* This column displays a description of the exercise for which the document has been submitted.

   ☐ *Document:* Click a document hyperlink to view your document using Paradigm Keyboarding's Word Processor.

Using the Paradigm Word Processor (PWP)

The Paradigm Word Processor (PWP) is a Web-based word processor that comes as part of PKB. To open PWP, take the following steps:

1. Click Word Processor on the PKB menu bar.

2. At the Paradigm Word Processor page, click the indicated hyperlink to launch PWP.

3. Click the Launch button at the Launch Word Processor dialog box that appears.

When you click the Launch button, a progress window is displayed while the necessary resource files are downloaded. Once the Word Processor application is launched, the progress window shuts down automatically.

Word Processor Functions and Commands

The following features, arranged by their location on PWP's pull-down menus, are available in the Paradigm Word Processor. Many of these features can also be accessed by keyboard commands (listed on the pull-down menus) or by buttons (a listing of which is found in a pull-out appendix at the back of your textbook):

File

* *New* – creates a new blank document.

* *Open* – opens a previously-created document. **Note:** PWP can only support one open document at a time.

* *Close* – closes the document currently on screen.

* *Save* – saves a document.

* *Save As* – brings up the *Save As* dialog box where you name and save a document.

* *Page Setup* – sets page size, margins, and regular tab stops. Printer Value gives minimum possible margins for selected printer.

* *Print Preview* – views whole page with margins sketched in. To view other pages, click the scroll arrows at the bottom right of the screen. To return to regular layout, repeat File→Print Preview to uncheck Print Preview. Print Preview also paginates documents for PWP. PWP does not support automatic pagination. This means that whenever you insert page breaks, you must select Print Preview to paginate the document.

- *Print* – prints current document.
- *Print Setup* – sets paper orientation and size, paper source, and printer.
- *Exit* – brings user back to the PKB Main Menu.

Edit

- *Undo* – removes last text typed. Will not remove any formatting.
- *Cut/Copy/Paste* – basic editing commands to remove, copy, or relocate selected text.
- *Clear* – removes selected text.
- *Select All* – highlights entire document.
- *Search* – finds, or finds and replaces, chosen text.

View

- *Hidden Characters* – select to view Paragraph Marks, Tab Characters, Spaces, or all three of these in a document.
- *Fields* – select to view Visible and/or Field Codes, such as page numbers.
- *Picture Place Holders* – select to view place holders of images inserted into the document.
- *Gridlines* – select to view gridlines for tables. This command is duplicated by the Table→Gridlines command.
- *Fit to Screen* – select to view text formatted to fit to screen. See note below on viewing and printing.
- *Unit* – select to view page ruler in cm (centimeters) or in (inches).
- *Header and Footer* – select to view header and footer for formatting and entering text. **Note:** No blank lines are inserted between the header and the body of a document; these must be added manually.

Insert

- *File* – inserts another file into an existing document.
- *Field* – inserts a field, such as a page number, into a document.
- *Picture* – inserts a Windows metafile image into a document.

- *Table* – creates a table with a selected number of columns and rows.

- *Symbol* – brings up a symbol screen, from which you can choose symbols to insert into a document. **Note:** After inserting a symbol, you must select the font you were using for text from the style bar, or the symbol font will remain the chosen font.

- *Page Break* – inserts a page break without waiting for the end of the page. To remove the page break, highlight the paragraph mark denoting the page break, and use the Cut or Clear Edit command to remove it. **Note:** You will need to use Print Preview to repaginate the document.

Format

- *Character* – formats text with the following choices: Normal, Bold, Underline, Italic, Strikeout, Superscript, Subscript, Font (includes size), and Color. Choosing one or more of these options will change the highlighted text or, if no text is highlighted, the subsequent typed text.

- *Paragraph* – formats Indents and Spacing by choosing indents, text alignment, and line spacing or Tabulators by setting tab stops (which can also be set on the page ruler using the mouse).

- *Tabs* – brings up same screen as *Paragraph*. Can choose to format Tabulators or Indents and Spacing.

- *Bullets and Numbering* – formats lists or outlines automatically using a selection of bullets or numbering formats.

Table

- *Insert Table* – creates a table with a selected number of columns and rows. This command is duplicated under Insert→Table.

- *Select Table* – highlights an entire table.

- *Insert Row/Delete Row/Select Row* – inserts, deletes, or highlights the row where the insertion point is currently located.

- *Insert Column/Delete Column* – inserts or deletes the column where the insertion point is currently located.

- *Insert Cells/Delete Cells* – inserts or deletes cells in the row where the insertion point is currently located.

- *Merge Cells* – merges highlighted cells.

- *Split Cells* – splits the cell where the insertion point is currently located. Prompt asks for number of cells desired.

- *Cell Height and Width* – adjusts the height of rows and the width of columns. **Note:** There is no auto-format feature in PWP. When you change the number of columns in a table, you must adjust the column width manually for the table to continue to fit the page width.

- *Borders and Shading* – formats table to show varying weights of gridlines and varying shades of coloring of the cells of the table. Also gives three-dimensional border options.

- *Gridlines* – shows the gridlines of a table. This command is duplicated by the View→Gridlines command. These gridlines are not visible on the printout unless borders are formatted for the table.

Viewing Your Syllabus

You can view a week-by-week syllabus for the Paradigm Keyboarding textbooks by clicking Syllabus on your PKB menu bar. To view the weekly session details for a book, select any book from the drop-down list and click Go.

Using Help/Contacting Your Instructor

You can access Help by clicking Help on the upper right corner of your screen. This help feature was created to provide you with a brief description on how to use Paradigm Keyboarding's menu system. Each of the menu items has been listed as they appear on the site, with the sub-menus covered as subtopics.

You can contact your instructor via e-mail by pointing to Profile on the PKB menu bar and clicking Instructor Details.